This Book Belongs to
Jack Jackter Elementary
School   2004-2005

Water
as a Solid

by Helen Frost

Consulting Editor: Gail Saunders-Smith, Ph.D.

Reviewer: Carolyn M. Tucker
Water Education Specialist
California Department of Water Resources

Pebble Books

an imprint of Capstone Press
Mankato, Minnesota

Pebble Books are published by Capstone Press
818 North Willow Street, Mankato, Minnesota 56001
http://www.capstone-press.com

Library of Congress Cataloging-in-Publication Data
Frost, Helen, 1949–
    Water as a solid/by Helen Frost.
    p. cm.—(Water)
    Includes bibliographical references and index.
    Summary: Simple text presents facts about water in its solid state, its properties,
and its uses.
    ISBN 0-7368-0411-0
    1. Ice—Juvenile literature. [1. Ice. 2. Snow. 3. Water.] I. Title. II. Series: Frost,
Helen, 1949– Water.
QC926.37.F76   2000
551.31—dc21
                                                                        99-14302
                                                                        CIP

Note to Parents and Teachers

The Water series supports national science standards for understanding the properties of water. This book describes and illustrates water as a solid. The photographs support early readers in understanding the text. The repetition of words and phrases helps early readers learn new words. This book also introduces early readers to subject-specific vocabulary words, which are defined in the Words to Know section. Early readers may need assistance to read some words and to use the Table of Contents, Words to Know, Read More, Internet Sites, and Index/Word List sections of the book.

Table of Contents

Water can be a liquid,
a gas, or a solid.
Water is a solid when
it is very cold.

Water freezes into
different shapes.
Frozen water is ice.

Ice cubes are small pieces of ice. Icebergs are huge pieces of ice.

Hail is a kind of ice
that falls from clouds.
Hail can be big or
small. Hail is hard.

Snow is a kind of
ice that falls from
clouds. Snow is soft.

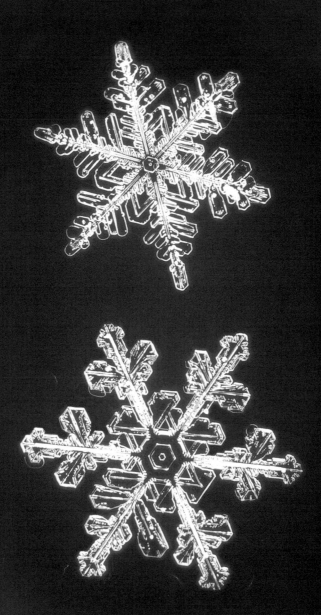

14

Snowflakes are ice crystals. Each snowflake has a different pattern.

Frost is ice crystals. Frost forms on cold surfaces.

18

Ice that melts and freezes again can make icicles. Icicles are long and pointed.

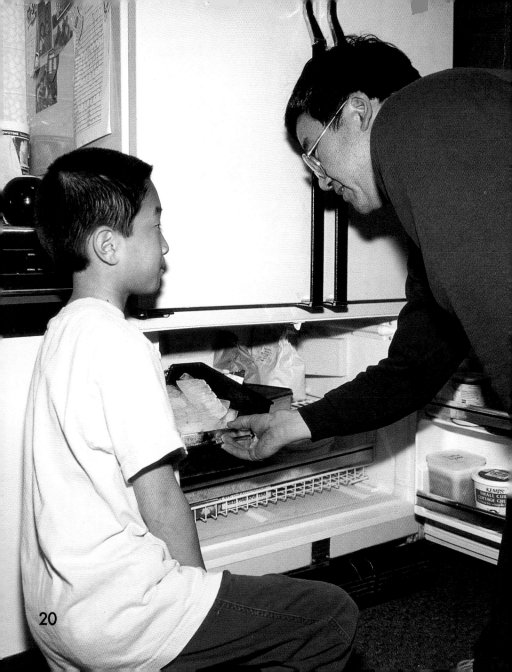

People use ice. Ice keeps food cold.

Words to Know

crystal—a solid made of small parts that form a pattern; snowflakes and frost are ice crystals.

frozen—being cold enough to turn from a liquid into a solid; ice is frozen water.

hail—balls of ice that form in clouds and fall to the ground; hail is made of layers of ice.

iceberg—a huge piece of ice that floats in the ocean; icebergs break off from glaciers.

icicle—a long, thin piece of ice that forms when ice melts, drips, and then freezes; icicles also form when flowing water freezes.

snow—crystals of ice; snow forms when water vapor freezes in the air.

solid—something that holds its shape; ice is the solid form of water; water freezes into a solid when it reaches 32 degrees Fahrenheit (0 degree Celsius).

Read More

Davies, Kay and Wendy Oldfield. *Snow and Ice.* See for Yourself. Austin, Texas: Raintree Steck-Vaughn, 1996.

Schaefer, Lola M. *A Snowy Day.* What Kind of Day Is It? Mankato, Minn.: Pebble Books, 2000.

Wick, Walter. *A Drop of Water: A Book of Science and Wonder.* New York: Scholastic, 1997.

Internet Sites

Ice and Snow
http://miavx1.muohio.edu/dragonfly/snow

Questions and Answers about Snow
http://bipolar.colorado.edu/NSIDC/ EDUCATION/SNOW/snow_FAQ.html

Snow Science
http://www.teelfamily.com/activities/snow/ science.html

Index/Word List

Word Count: 113
Early-Intervention Level: 13

Editorial Credits

Mari C. Schuh, editor; Timothy Halldin, cover designer; Kimberly Danger, photo researcher

Photo Credits

Brian Parker/TOM STACK & ASSOCIATES, 1
David F. Clobes, 8 (top), 20
International Stock/Warren Faidley, 10 (both)
James P. Rowan, 4, 8 (bottom)
Photo Network/Henryk T. Kaiser, 18
Robert McCaw, 16
Shaffer Photography/James L. Shaffer, cover, 6
Thomas Kitchin/TOM STACK & ASSOCIATES, 12
Visuals Unlimited/Richard C. Walters, 14